HISTORIC PHOTOS OF THE
CANADIAN ROCKIES

Summerthought

Banff, Alberta

HISTORIC PHOTOS OF THE CANADIAN ROCKIES

Published by

Summerthought

Summerthought Publishing
PO Box 2309
Banff, AB T1L 1C1
Canada
www.summerthought.com

Printing History
1st Edition—2008

Library and Archives Canada Cataloguing in Publication

Historic Photos of the Canadian Rockies/edited by Andrew Hempstead.

Includes bibliographical references and index.

ISBN 978-0-9782375-6-1

1. Rocky Mountains, Canadian (B.C. and Alta.)—History—Pictorial works. I. Hempstead, Andrew

FC219.H58 2008   971.10022'2   C2008-901175-9

Design and production: Linda Petras
Printed in Canada by Friesens

Contents

A diver plunges into the Terrace Pool at the Chateau Lake Louise.

Introduction

Beautiful lakes, snowcapped peaks, endless glaciers and icefields, colourful alpine meadows, and an abundance of wildlife. While these are the elements the Canadian Rockies are best known for, the region also has a colourful and intriguing human history that has been recorded in various mediums.

Human habitation of the Canadian Rockies began long before the first Europeans arrived. It is thought the Kootenay (also spelt Kootenai) were the first human beings to arrive in the Canadian Rockies, entering the Columbia River Valley around 10,000 years ago and crossing the mountains to hunt on the Kootenay Plains. The movement of humans into the mountains from the east was much more recent, with Assiniboine (known today as Stoney) people reaching the foothills region a few hundred years ago. While pictographs created by these earliest visitors are the only visual record of pre-European contact, early photographers found willing models in the Stoney and many photographic images from the late 1800s and early 1900s reflect the traditions and customs of these people.

In 1754, from a ridge near present Red Deer, Anthony Henday became the first white man to view the Canadian Rockies. In 1807, David Thompson crossed the mountains by travelling up the North Saskatchewan River from Rocky Mountain House, and descending from Howse Pass to the Columbia River. A half-century later, Captain John Palliser explored many of the watersheds leading into the mountains, including one trip up the Bow River and over Vermilion Pass. While there is no photographic record of these expeditions, it was these earliest explorers that opened up the region to those that would follow.

A Stoney family photographed by Mary Shäffer, who spent much of her life exploring, photographing, and writing about the Canadian Rockies.

Many of the earliest European settlements in the Canadian Rockies predated widespread use of cameras, including fur trading posts at Rocky Mountain House, where just chimneys remained when this photograph was taken in 1905. A succession of posts established at Rocky Mountain House as early as 1799 were used for not only trading, but also as bases for exploring the Canadian Rockies.

Naturally occurring changes to the landscape of the Canadian Rockies over the last century have been a lot more subtle than those made by humans, but by looking back at early photographs changes can be seen. In this 1927 photograph, it is easy to see how Angel Glacier, in Jasper National Park, received its name. Since then, the glacier has receded greatly and is now "wing-less."

Railway crew on hand car, 1888.

Trains

In the 1860s, with a movement to push for Canadian independence gaining ground, the British government passed legislation establishing the Dominion of Canada. At that time, life in the North-West Territories, as most of what is now western Canada was then known, was primitive. There were no laws, and no outpost held more than a couple of dozen residents. In an effort to solidify the region's British sovereignty, British Columbia joined the Dominion on the condition that the federal government committed to building a railway to link the fledgling province with the rest of the country. While it proved to be an essential ingredient to the success of settling the West, a railway was mostly regarded by the eastern provinces as unnecessary and uneconomical.

Many routes across the Canadian Rockies were considered by the Canadian Pacific Railway, but Kicking Horse Pass, surveyed by Major A. B. Rogers in 1881, got the final nod. The rail line and its construction camps pushed into the mountains from the east, reaching Siding 29 (known today as Banff) early in the fall of 1883, Holt City (Lake Louise) a couple of months later, then crossing the Continental Divide and reaching what is now the village of Field in the summer of 1884. The following year, on November 7, 1885, the final spike was laid west of Rogers Pass at Craigellachie, opening up the lanes of commerce between British Columbia and the rest of the Canada. A second, more northerly route through Edmonton and Jasper, was completed by the Grand Trunk Pacific Railway in 1914.

With two expensive rail lines in place, the government set about putting them to use by settling the land and encouraging tourists to visit the thriving resort towns of Banff and Jasper. Roads were built and industries—including logging, mining, farming, and tourism—started to develop.

As the railway pushed westward into the Canadian Rockies, the first major divisional point was Canmore, which was named for a Scottish town. By 1886, a ramshackle community had been established along the tracks (pictured), but at this time there was no hint at the riches of coal that would see the town thrive in later years.

Banff Railway Station as it looked in 1888, the year the Banff Springs Hotel opened.

Banff Railway Station continued to be an important part of town life for many decades, and the only link to the outside world.

When construction of the transcontinental rail line reached what is now Lake Louise in 1884, a rough-and-tumble construction camp known as "Holt City" sprang up in the wilderness.

Holt City became known as Laggan in 1885 (above). Word of the surrounding beauty soon spread and various businesses were established along the valley floor. In 1910, the Canadian Pacific Railway built a more permanent railway station (below), one that still stands today. The name of the community was officially changed from Laggan to Lake Louise in 1914.

West of Lake Louise, the original rail line had a gradient of 4.5% as it descended from Kicking Horse Pass. After two decades, this treacherous stretch of track was replaced by the famous Spiral Tunnels, which were completed in 1909 after three years of construction. The new routing comprised two tunnels that looped through Cathedral Mountain and Mount Ogden. The tunnels made a circular route, emerging around 20 meters (66 feet) below the point where they entered the mountains, and thereby reducing the gradient by half.

As construction of the rail line continued westward across the Canadian Rockies, camps were erected to house and feed railway workers. One such settlement was Field, which was named for Cyrus Field, sponsor of the first transatlantic communication cable.

Kicking Horse Pass was only one of the hurdles for railway engineers. Further west, constructing a rail line through Kicking Horse Canyon proved to be just as challenging.

Immediately west of the Canadian Rockies, the rugged Selkirk Mountains provided yet more challenges for railway engineers and workers. The Mountain Creek Bridge, one of eight bridges through these mountains, needed around two million board feet of lumber and was at the time one of the world's largest wooden structures.

Jasper had already been declared a park when the Grand Trunk Pacific Railway was constructed as a rival to the more southern Canadian Pacific Railway. It crossed the park in 1911, with Summit City (pictured) housing workers at the Yellowhead Pass.

For the first decades of the last century, tourists arrived in Jasper by train, at this railway station that still serves as a stop on the transcontinental rail line.

Various mining operations through the Canadian Rockies relied on the railway for transportation. A concentration of mines were in the Kicking Horse Valley, where lead and zinc were extracted from high on the slopes of Mt. Stephen and transported to the valley floor in small coal cars. Pictured is the precarious access road to one of these mines, the Monarch, which began operation in 1912.

Rotary snowplows, similar to the one pictured above, were developed to help clear the snow, which quickly accumulated through the winter months. When this proved inadequate, expensive "snow sheds" (opposite) in the Selkirk Mountains, were constructed where snowfall and avalanche risk were highest.

In an effort to recoup some of the money spent in laying the railway through the Canadian Rockies, William Cornelius Van Horne, general manager of the Canadian Pacific Railway, ordered construction of dining rooms and hotels to serve visitors using the railway. One of these was Mount Stephen House, in Field, which was completed in 1886. It was luxurious in all respects—from its elegant gas lights to fine china—but unlike hotels in Banff and Lake Louise, no longer exists.

Another dining room no longer in existence is Glacier House, at Rogers Pass, which was built in 1886 as a place where trains could stop to allow travellers to have a meal. Eventually rooms were added allowing for overnight stays. In this image (right), staff from Glacier House pose for the photographer.

While some railway construction camps evolved into bustling towns, others, such as Moberly House at the mouth of the Blaeberry River near present-day Golden, were abandoned as soon as workers moved on.

Engine 316 at Donald, British Columbia in 1887. Donald, west of Golden, was originally a divisional point for the Canadian Pacific Railway, but was abandoned for Revelstoke less than a decade after the railway was completed. Those interested in the history of train travel in the Canadian Rockies will enjoy visits to the nearby Revelstoke Railway Museum and Cranbrook's Canadian Museum of Rail Travel.

Illecillewaet, once a bustling town, has long since disappeared.

Towns

In the late 1880s, after the Canadian Pacific Railway had been completed, the Canadian Rockies region was a vast wilderness accessible only by rail. The parks and the landscape they encompassed were considered economic resources to be exploited rather than as national treasures to be preserved. Logging, hunting, and mining were permitted inside park boundaries; all but Kootenay National Park had mines operating within them for many years (the last mine, in Yoho National Park, closed in 1952). Today, five national parks protect much of the Canadian Rockies, with the towns of Banff and Jasper at the heart of their respectively named parks.

Many of the region's earliest towns were built around mining operations, including Bankhead, Anthracite, Pocahontas, and Oil City, all of which have long since disappeared. Canmore, on the other hand, where mining began in 1887, continues to thrive. The region's most famous town, Banff, was developed around hot springs that had been discovered by railway workers. With the idea of developing a European-style spa resort, the government surveyed a townsite and encouraged the CPR to build a world-class hotel. Meanwhile to the north, the town of Jasper started as a construction camp, but became popular as a tourist destination in the early 1900s.

Banff Avenue, 1887.

After being surveyed in 1886, Banff Avenue became the town's main street. The first buildings were simple wood-frame structures with false fronts. One such business was Wilson & Fear, one of the town's many "curio stores" that stocked a wide range of merchandise (below) appealing to both locals and tourists.

Banff's first post office was this primitive log cabin on the east side of Banff Avenue that operated through the 1890s.

Lake Minnewanka has always been a popular spot for Banff locals in summer. A hotel was built beside the lake in 1886 and by 1912, when this photo is dated, streets had been laid out at the "Summer Village" and tour boats were operating up and down the lake (opposite). When the present dam was built in 1941, the townsite was flooded, leaving the village nothing but a memory that is today only visited by divers.

The Banff Winter Carnival was devised as a way to keep the locals entertained during winter and also to attract tourists in the off-season. A highlight was an Ice Palace on Banff Avenue (opposite, top) while ski jumping, ski racing, figure-skating (above), and cross-country skiing attracted competitors from throughout the region. Other carnival spectacles became annual traditions including a toboggan run extending from Tunnel Mountain to the Bow River and ice carving (opposite).

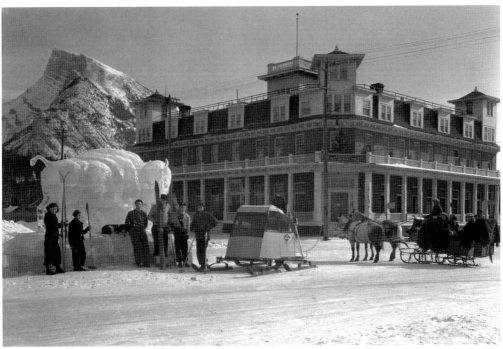

In March 1929, two Banff boys, Cliff White and Cyril Paris, returned from an area known as Sunshine with stories of deep snow and excellent skiing conditions. In the ensuing years, many locals followed in their footsteps and by 1934 paying guests were staying in a small log cabin overlooking the best runs.

The town of Banff has always been a popular stop for celebrities and royalty, including King George VI and Queen Elizabeth, who stayed at the Banff Springs Hotel in 1939. Jim Brewster, who was assigned as their chauffeur, invited the royal couple to stop by his home for afternoon tea, to which they kindly agreed. Local legend has it that Jim failed to inform his wife of the plan, and arrived unannounced with the King and Queen of England.

This 1889 photo looking south across Canmore from the hoodoos shows early town buildings concentrated along the railway line. Canmore's first coal mine began operation two years earlier on the south side of the river.

Looking east across Canmore in the early 1900s. The railway bridge in the foreground, now part of the local trail system, was used to transport coal from the mines to the main Canadian Pacific Railway line.

The Shareholders Cabin was built in 1914 as a place for mine shareholders to stay when they visited Canmore. Having undergone extensive renovations, this impressive log building still stands in a prime location across the Bow River from downtown.

By 1900, Canmore had its own hockey team (above) and even a brass band (below).

Canada Day has always been a popular event in Canmore. This photo shows the 1925 parade.

Canmore's Three Sisters remain a local landmark, well over a century since this photo was taken in the 1880s.

Looking across to the Three Sisters from the Bow Valley Trail in the 1920s.

Jasper House, as photographed by surveyor Charles Horetzky in 1872. Operated by Jasper Hawes for the Hudson's Bay Company, this remote trading post was located along the Athabasca River east of present-day Jasper. It served as an important stopping place for traders and explorers from 1825 until a couple of years after this photograph was taken.

In 1910, the Grand Trunk Pacific Railway chose the present-day site of Jasper as a major station and divisional point. Stores were opened, accommodation built for park staff, and by 1914, when the rail line was completed, the town had a population of 125.

Jasper Fire Hall and firemen in 1915

Now home to the Jasper Visitor Centre, the Park Administration Building is a local landmark. Designed by architect A. M. Calderon and completed in 1914, it was built using local materials and intended to give a positive first impression for rail travellers who alighted from the nearby railway station.

Rodeos aren't usually associated with the Canadian Rockies, but the Jasper Rodeo has been a popular gathering in that town since the inaugural event in 1926. Pictured is Slim Henry riding Skyhigh to first place in the 1937 rodeo.

This 1926 streetscape depicts Jasper's main thoroughfare, which by that time had a permanent look. The second building from the left was originally owned by the Jackman family and is now home to Jasper Camera and Gift.

By 1930, Jasper as a town had taken shape, with streets laid out as you find them today.

A prospector at Golden in 1884. Unlike the name may suggest, there never has been any gold found at Golden. Instead, the town's name was coined in an attempt to outshine a townsite to the east which had called itself "Silver City."

Unlike many other construction camps along the Canadian Pacific Railway, Golden thrived long after itinerant construction workers had moved on. The most important local industry was logging, with lumber processed at mills along the valley floor.

Downtown Golden as photographed by Byron Harmon in 1931.

Once a bustling town on the northern shore of Lake Windermere, Athalmer has long since been lost to time, although the original railway station is preserved at Windermere Valley Museum, which overlooks the former townsite.

What is most striking about this aerial photograph looking north across Invermere is the date—it was taken as recently as 1968.

John George "Kootenai" Brown acquired his nickname through close association with the Kootenay (today's preferred spelling) people, hunting buffalo and wolves with them until the animals had all but disappeared. Brown built a cabin by Upper Waterton Lake in 1869, becoming the valley's first permanent resident. When a reserve was set aside in 1895, Brown was employed as its first warden. In 1911, the area was declared a national park and Brown, age 71, was appointed its superintendent. He continued to push for an expansion of park boundaries until his final retirement at age 75.

The short-lived Rocky Mountain Development Company, which struck oil in what is now Waterton Lakes National Park in 1901, was the first producing oil well in western Canada.

Looking across Upper Waterton Lake in 1935, with the silhouette of the Prince of Wales Hotel clearly visible.

Many towns through the Canadian Rockies have disappeared. Some began as rough-and-tumble mining camps, including Anthracite, a coal-mining town between present-day Banff and Canmore. It flourished between 1896 and 1904, with a population that peaked at around 300.

Along what is now Lake Minnewanka Road in Banff National Park, Bankhead was once a thriving coal-mining town of 1,000 residents. Coal was extracted from the mid-slopes of Cascade Mountain and transported by coal cars to the valley floor, where this tipple (above) sorted and processed the raw ore. When the mine closed in 1922, all the buildings were moved or demolished. Some foundations remain, include those of Holy Trinity Church, which can be seen in the distance in this 1910 photo (below).

A plaque beside the Bow Valley Parkway marks the site of Silver City, once a boomtown of 2,000 in the shadow of Castle Mountain. In the 1880s, five mines were operating and the town itself boasted a half-dozen hotels, four or five stores, two real-estate offices, and a station on the transcontinental rail line. But the boom was short-lived. Two men, named Patton and Pettigrew, salted their mine with gold and silver ore to attract investors. After selling 2,000 shares at $5 each, they vanished, leaving investors with a useless mine. Investment in the town ceased, mines closed, and the people left. Only one man refused to leave. His name was James Smith (pictured), but he was known to everyone as Joe. In 1887, when Silver City came under the jurisdiction of the National Parks Service, Joe was allowed to remain—and he did so until 1937, when he was finally persuaded to move to a Calgary retirement home.

When gold was discovered along Wild Horse Creek in 1865, the Columbia Valley was flooded with hopeful miners. The town of Fort Steele grew to be the largest in the valley, its main street (pictured in 1898) lined with businesses that have been re-created at today's Fort Steele Heritage Town, north of Cranbrook.

Women skiers at Jasper

Tourism

With an expensive rail line in place, the Canadian Pacific Railway began encouraging visitors to the mountains by building grand mountain resorts: Mount Stephen House in 1886, the Banff Springs Hotel in 1888, a lodge at Lake Louise in 1890, and Emerald Lake Lodge in 1902. Knowledgeable locals, some of whom had been used as guides and outfitters during railway construction, offered their services to the tourists the railway brought. Tom Wilson, Bill Peyto, Jimmy Simpson, and Jim and Bill Brewster are synonymous with this era, and their names grace everything from pubs to mountain peaks.

Recreational mountaineering has been popular in the Canadian Rockies since the late 1800s, when European and American alpinists began making first ascents. Many early climbers were inexperienced and ill-equipped, but first ascents were nevertheless made on peaks that today are still considered difficult. In 1894, Walter Wilcox and Samuel Allen, two Yale schoolmates, spent the summer climbing in the Lake Louise area, making successful first ascents of Mount Temple and Mount Aberdeen, extraordinary achievements considering their lack of experience and proper equipment. After Philip Stanley Abbot became North America's first mountaineering fatality in 1896, the Canadian Pacific Railway began employing Swiss guides to make the sport safer.

One of the major changes that has occurred since the first tourists began arriving in the Canadian Rockies is the way the complex relationship between humans and wildlife has been managed. Today, the trend favours the wildlife, but early in the history of the Canadian Rockies' parks, the operating strategy clearly favoured the visitor, as you will discover in this chapter.

On November 8, 1883, three workers—Franklin McCabe and William and Thomas McCardell—went prospecting for gold on their day off from construction of the rail line through the Bow Valley. After crossing the Bow River by raft, they came across a warm stream and traced it to its source at a small basin of warm water. Nearby, they detected a sulphurous smell permeating from a hole in the ground. Nervously, one of the three men lowered himself into the hole and came across a subterranean pool of aqua-green warm water. The three men had found not gold, but something just as precious—a hot mineral spring that in time would attract wealthy customers from around the world. Word of the discovery soon got out, and the government encouraged visitors to the Cave and Basin (pictured opposite in 1890) as a source of revenue to support the new railway.

Lifeguards at the Cave and Basin, circa 1930.

Radium Hot Springs, in Kootenay National Park, was discovered many centuries ago by the Kootenay people, who, like today's visitors, came to enjoy the hot, odourless water that gushes out of the ground. Originally known as Sinclair Hot Springs, Englishman Roland Stuart purchased the springs for $160 in 1890 and built rough concrete pools to contain the water. Today the water is diverted from its natural course into the commercial pools, including one that is Canada's largest.

Miette Hot Springs was a major attraction for early tourists visiting Jasper National Park. In 1910, a packhorse trail was built up to the remote springs and a bathhouse was constructed (pictured). The original hand-hewn log structure was replaced in the 1930s with pools that remained in use until new facilities were built in 1985.

Known as "the Castle,"
the Banff Springs Hotel
(pictured in 1888) is one
of the world's great
mountain resorts.

Dr. Robert G. Brett, a medical practitioner for the Canadian Pacific Railway, saw the potential for a health resort affiliated with the hot springs and opened the Banff Sanitarium in 1887. It was renamed Hotel Bretton Hall in 1922 but burned down in 1933. Today, the Park Administration Building stands on the site.

Few guides in Banff were as well known as Jim (right) and Bill Brewster. In 1892, before they were even teenagers, they were hired by the Banff Springs Hotel to take guests to local attractions. As their reputation as guides grew, they built a thriving business. By 1900, they had their own livery and outfitting company (below). Their other business interests included a trading post, the original Mount Royal Hotel, a ski lodge in Sunshine Meadows, and the hotel at the Columbia Icefield.

Fishing in the Bow River, 1890.

In 1894, heavy rains washed out several railway bridges, halting train traffic in Banff. To entertain stranded travellers, Stoney people from nearby Morley were bought in to put on a dance demonstration. The event proved so popular that they were invited back for Dominion Day until 1907 when Banff Indian Days was launched as its own annual event. A colourful parade along Banff Avenue (above) marked the beginning of several days of singing, dancing, and native athletic competitions.

The first accommodation at Lake Louise was a simple log cabin that opened for guests in 1890. It featured a veranda, sitting room, kitchen, and one bedroom. In its early years less than 100 guests—mostly climbers and artists—would visit over the entire summer season.

The much-expanded Lake Louise Chalet as it looked in the early 1900s.

In 1909, two Tudor-style, timber wings were added, increasing capacity to 240 guests.

Constructed in the 1920s by the Canadian Pacific Railway, Plain of the Six Glaciers Teahouse still operates today—serving light refreshments to hikers who make the long trek up from Lake Louise.

As the automobile gained popularity in the 1920s, accommodations were built specifically to cater to visitors who arrived by motor vehicle. Typically, they consisted of a cluster of cabins set around a central lodge where meals were served and—with no need for the railway—were spread throughout the Canadian Rockies. Many of these still operate while others, such as Mount Edith Cavell Chalet in Jasper National Park (pictured), have been demolished.

One of the most beautiful lakes in the Canadian Rockies is Moraine Lake. Within a decade of its discovery by Walter Wilcox in 1899, a trail from Lake Louise had been constructed and a teahouse built on the lakeshore. In 1922, cabins were built, with more added through the years. In 1988, architect Arthur Erickson transformed the complex into elegant Moraine Lake Lodge, one of the world's great mountain retreats.

Construction of the mountainous Icefields Parkway between Lake Louise and Jasper began in 1931, with crews working toward each other from both ends. The ambitious 230-kilometre (143-mile)-long project was completed in 1939. Today's Icefields Parkways follows much of the original roadbed, and was paved in the late 1950s. Travellers still enjoy the same spectacular mountain scenery as early travelers, including views across to Mt. Temple (left) and north to distinctive Mt. Chephren (below).

When it was built by legendary mountain man Jimmy Simpson in the 1920s, Num-Ti-Jah Lodge, on the shore of Bow Lake, was only accessible by horse from Lake Louise. When the Icefields Parkway reach Bow Lake in 1937, Simpson began upgrading the lodge with more rooms and a distinctive log and stone exterior that remains as appealing today as it did over 70 years ago.

The Swiss-influenced Columbia Icefield Chalet opened in 1940 (pictured), with early tourists exploring the nearby Athabasca Glacier on horseback.

Sunwapta Falls, pictured in the 1920s, has always been a popular natural attraction for visitors to Jasper National Park.

THE LOUNGE. JASPER PARK LODGE.

In the same traditions as the Banff Springs Hotel, Jasper Park Lodge has been the premier accommodation in that park since it opened in 1921. The original resort comprised a single-storey structure, reputed to be the largest log building in the world, surrounded by log bungalows. In the main building was a lounge (pictured) and dining room.

Construction of the Banff-Windermere Highway through the rugged terrain of Kootenay National Park took almost a decade. Near Radium Hot Springs, Sinclair Canyon (pictured) had been eroded by the fast-flowing waters of Sinclair Creek, but was not wide enough for the road. After dynamiting the canyon and building the road over the top of the creek, the gap was wide enough for the two-lane highway as it exists today.

Originally known as the Kicking Horse Trail, a road through Yoho National Park was completed in 1926 (above), but it wasn't until 1958 that the route was officially recognized. It is now the Trans-Canada Highway, although much of the original roadbed within the park has been bypassed, including the bridge in Kicking Horse Canyon pictured below.

Scenery is only part of the fun for drivers traversing the Yoho Valley Road. Engineers were forced to include two very tight switchbacks that to this day force buses to reverse through the mid-section.

Snowfall is high in the Yoho Valley. Instead of waiting for the snow to melt, a tunnel would be cleared through the snow to allow vehicles to reach Takakkaw Falls in spring.

A lodge has existed at Emerald Lake since 1902. The original framework of the building pictured is used in today's main lodge, which is now surrounded by upscale chalets.

Waterton's best-known landmark, the Prince of Wales Hotel, is a seven-storey gabled structure that has changed little in appearance since it took its first guests in 1927. It was another grand mountain resort financed by a railway, except, unlike those in Banff and Jasper, it had no rail link. It was built as part of a chain of lodgings in Glacier National Park, with early guests transported to the hotel by bus from the Great Northern Railway in Montana.

The Akamina Parkway is one of the few roads penetrating Waterton Lakes National Park. Constructed in the 1920s, it allowed visitors to easily reach Cameron Lake, where fishing was the most popular activity.

A rescue party rests (above) while retrieving the body of Philip Stanley Abbot. On August 4, 1896, Abbot became North America's first climbing fatality. After his untimely death, the Canadian Pacific Railway hired Swiss mountaineers (below) as a way to promote adventure tourism and to ensure the safety of visitors. Based at mountain hotels in Banff, Lake Louise, Golden, and Rogers Pass, these guides made hundreds of first ascents in the Canadian Rockies.

Conrad Kain pictured leading a party to the summit of Mount Resplendent in 1913. Kain, an Austrian, was an official guide for the Alpine Club of Canada. He was credited with around 50 first ascents in the Canadian Rockies and Selkirk Mountains, but is best known as the first to reach the summit of Mount Robson, the highest mountain in the Canadian Rockies.

Swiss Guide Rudolf Aemmer was employed as a guide at Lake Louise between 1909 and 1949.

In 1923, an eclectic group of outdoor enthusiasts—including noted wildlife artist Carl Rungius and Dr. Charles D. Walcott, secretary of the Smithsonian Institute—set off on an organized horseback ride to help promote the Canadian Rockies. Known today as the Trail Riders of the Canadian Rockies, the non-profit organization continues to thrive. Like they have for over 80 years, riders camp in tepees, feast on hearty camp cooking, and enjoy western-style entertainment, such as that provided in 1935 by Wilf Carter (pictured).

A 1914 Alpine Club of Canada outing silhouetted against the Yoho Glacier.

Employed by the Canadian Pacific Railway on an early survey team, Tom Wilson is credited with being the first non-native to set eyes on Lake Louise. He went on to operate a successful outfitting business, exploring the Yoho Valley and the area around Mount Assiniboine, while also mentoring the likes of Bill Peyto and Jimmy Simpson. After officially retiring, he was employed by the Banff Springs Hotel to entertain guests with stories from the "old days."

One of the Canadian Rockies' greatest guides and also one of the region's most infamous characters was Bill Peyto, whose distinctive dress sense—a tilted sombrero, fringed buckskin coat, cartridge belt, hunting knife, and six-shooter—had him looking more like a gunslinger than a mountain man.

Jack Giddie, a park warden, atop Mount Burgess in Yoho National Park, 1924.

One of the earliest movies shot in the Canadian Rockies was the 1922 drama *Valley of the Silent Men,* starring Lew Cody. It was mostly filmed on Tunnel Mountain, near where the campground now lies.

The stunning scenery of the Canadian Rockies has been showcased in films starring some of the world's greatest movie stars (think Brad Pitt in *The Assassination of Jesse James by the Coward Robert Ford*), even if the finished product was forgettable (Russell Crowe in *Mystery, Alaska,* or Anthony Hopkins and Alec Baldwin in *The Edge*), but it was Marilyn Monroe and Robert Mitchum that really got the locals talking while filming *River of No Return* though Banff and Jasper National Parks in 1953. Monroe is pictured here at Becker's Chalets, in Jasper, after spraining her ankle on the set.

Tourists visiting the Canadian Rockies in the early 1900s were eager to see wildlife without actually having to venture into the wilderness. To fill this need, the Government Museum, filled with taxidermied animals, was constructed on Banff Avenue. Adjacent to the museum was the Banff Zoo, which kept more than 60 species of animals. The zoo is long gone, but the museum, now operating as the Banff Park Museum, is an interesting link to the park's past.

Many animals were caged at the Animal Paddock, at the base of Cascade Mountain, including this cougar, photographed in 1907.

Beside the Animal Paddock was the Buffalo Paddock, which was built to enclose a herd of bison, including "Sir Donald" (right). A small herd of buffalo remained until 1997, when the fences were removed to create a wildlife corridor.

In addition to the changing needs of park visitors, over the last century human-wildlife relationships are now managed very differently. For a long time, feeding bears was considered part of the "wilderness" experience, and as recently as the 1960s, tourists were encouraged to watch bears feast on garbage at local dumps.

Elliott Barnes in his cabin on the Kootenay Plains.

About the Photographers

The images in this book were created by a vast number of photographers. Following is a brief biography of those whose work appears most often.

Elliott Barnes (1866-1938)

Born in Rochester, New York, Barnes began his career photographing in Colorado and Wyoming before immigrating to Canada in 1905. He settled on the Kootenay Plains and continued to photograph while operating an outfitting business for clients visiting Banff. Later in his career, Barnes upgraded to a large format Graflex Speed Graphic camera, which was capable of producing custom postcards.

Boorne and May

With studios across what is now Alberta, Boorne and May was an esteemed photographic business that opened a studio in Calgary in 1886 and then expanded to Edmonton. The company was owned by two cousins, William Hanson Boorne and Ernest Gundry May, who photographed both in their studios and

around the region in what was then an almost uninhabited wilderness.

Byron Harmon (1876-1942)

Born in Washington state, Byron Harmon arrived in Banff in 1903 as an accomplished photographer. He began selling a line of postcards and as official photographer for the Alpine Club of Canada had a unique opportunity to photograph the Canadian Rockies from a

Byron Harmon

mountaineer's perspective. In addition to operating Byron Harmon Photos, Harmon opened a number of other businesses in Banff, including a drug store, theatre, and bookstore.

George Noble (1879-1965)

After apprenticing as a professional photographer in England, George Noble migrated to Canada and began a photographic business in a store owned by his uncles, George and Bill Fear (see page 30). After purchasing the business in 1932, Noble transformed the curio shop into a photographic studio, while also selling hand-coloured prints of local landmarks.

Vaux family

The three Vaux siblings—Mary (1860-1940), George (1863-1927), and William (1872-1908)—made their first trip to the Canadian Rockies in 1885 with their father, George Vaux VIII of Philadelphia. Family photographs record this trip, as well as a trip two years later along the Canadian Pacific Railway. The three children grew up to be accomplished photographers, scientists, and mountaineers, visiting the region frequently over the next two decades. William's work, which highlights glaciers, is of particular interest to scientists today as they study glacial advance and retreat.

Mary Vaux and guide on the Illecillewaet Glacier, 1905

Index

Photo Credits

Summerthought Publishing would like to thank the following for permission to reproduce their archival images:

BC Archives: p. 52 (i-51558); p. 53 (i-21500); p. 59 (b-09408).

Eleanor Luxton Historical Foundation: p. 32-33; p. 71; p. 97 lower.

Glenbow Archives: p. 10 (NA-1909-5); p. 11 top (NA-2977-1); p. 12 (NA-1432-17); p. 38 (NA-3740-5; William Notman); p. 42 top (NA-2536-10); p. 44 (NA-937-2; S.J. Thompson); p. 46 (NA-1408-19; Charles Horetzky); p. 47 top (NA-1679-12; Edgar Spurgeon); p. 54 (NA-678-1); p. 55 top (NA-1585-6); p. 65 (NA-3934-14); p. 66-67 (NA-1075-4); p. 72 (NA-2977-19); p. 84 (NB-32-7); p. 85 top (NB-32-33), lower (NA-4868-139).

Jasper-Yellowhead Museum & Archives: p. 18 lower (PA41-88); p. 47 lower (PA 18-3); p. 48 top (997.07.77.07), lower (89.36.262); p. 49 top (PA 18-22), lower (996.33.390); p. 60 (PA 101-3).

Whyte Museum of the Canadian Rockies: p. 4 (V263/NA-4910; Byron Harmon); p. 6 (V527/NG-124; Mary Shäffer); p. 7 top (V48/NA65-21; Elliott Barnes), lower (V492/NA66-1945); p. 8 (V10/NA66-680); p. 11 lower (V484/NA66-345); p. 13 top (NA66-392), lower (V653/NA-664); p. 14 (V653/NA-1609; Vaux family); p. 15 top (V10/NA66-650; Boorne and May); p. 15 lower (V265/NA66-267); p. 16-17 (V10/NA66-695; Boorne & May); p. 18 top (V263/NA-1157; Byron Harmon); p. 19 (V263/NA-0242; Byron Harmon); p. 20 (V138-lc-NA66-2471; William G. Barclay); p. 21 (V653/NG-255); p. 22 (V653/NG-737; Vaux family); p. 23 top (V653/NG-481; Vaux family), lower (NA66-236); p. 24 (V10/NA66-681; Boorne & May); p. 25 (V10/NA66-692; Boorne & May); p. 26 (V653/NA-103; Vaux family); p. 28-29 (V633/NA66-1796); p. 30 top (NA-529-20), lower (V653/NA80-67; Vaux family); p. 31 (V86/NA66-1788); p. 33 (V484/NA29-334); p. 34 (V469/1131; George Noble); p. 35 top (V469/1097; George Noble), lower (V263/NA-3392); p. 36 (V92/NA66-1873; Malcolm Meades); p. 37 (NA66-1488); p. 39 (NA66-162); p. 40-41 (V469/993; George Noble); p. 42 lower (V532/NA66-1888); p. 43 (NA66-134; Bert Prendergast); p. 45 (V469/2691; George Noble); p. 50 top (V701/LC-223), lower (V469/943; George Noble); p. 51 (V263/NA-5308); p. 55 lower (V91/NA66-2250); p. 56 (V653/NG-26; Vaux family); p. 57 top (V48/NA65-226), lower (NA66-459); p. 58 (NA66-453); p. 62 (V341/lc-NA66-1354; John Woodruff); p. 63 (V298-44); p. 64 (V469/955; George Noble); p. 68 (V469/1835); p. 69 top (V90/PC-1-NA66-1962), lower (V92/NG3-3); p. 70 (V341/lc-NA66-1359; John Woodruff); p. 73 top (V287/lc-NA66-2387), lower (V653/NA-1621; Vaux family); p. 74 (V469/2590; George Noble); p. 75 top (V492/NA66-1944), lower (V263/NA-5061; Byron Harmon); p. 76 (V469/2343; George Noble), lower (V469/479; George Noble); p. 77 top (V469/1002; George Noble); p. 78 top (V469/999; George Noble), lower (V469/1029; George Noble); p. 79 (NA66-2419; F.H. Slark); p. 80 (V469/618; George Noble); p. 81 top (V469/2044; George Noble), lower (V263/NA-5320; Byron Harmon); p. 82 (V263/NA-5235; Byron Harmon); p. 83 top (V469/931; George Noble), lower (V263/NA-5231; Byron Harmon); p. 86 top (V701/lc-5; Charles Thompson), lower (NA66-186); p. 87 (V263/NA-0936); p. 88 (V200/NA66-1818; Walter Wilcox); p. 89 (V226/lc-NA66-2407); p. 90 (V263/NA-153; Byron Harmon); p. 92 top (V701/LC-36); p. 92 lower (V85/NA66-577); p. 93 (V120/NA66-1767); p. 94 (PA139-347); p. 95 (V725/NA66-1673); p. 96 (V529/lc-3-NA66-198; Howard A. Chapman); p. 97 top (V48/427; Elliott Barnes); p. 98-99 (V469/1552; George Noble); p. 99 top (NA66-412), lower (NA66-413); p. 100 (V48/NG 9-2; Elliott Barnes); p. 101 (V263/NA-0408; Byron Harmon); p. 102 (V653/NA-1339; Vaux family).